Clownfish

by Lindsay Shaffer

BELLWETHER MEDIA • MINNEAPOLIS, MN

Note to Librarians, Teachers, and Parents:

Blastoff! Readers are carefully developed by literacy experts and combine standards-based content with developmentally appropriate text.

Level 1 provides the most support through repetition of high-frequency words, light text, predictable sentence patterns, and strong visual support.

Level 2 offers early readers a bit more challenge through varied simple sentences, increased text load, and less repetition of high-frequency words.

Level 3 advances early-fluent readers toward fluency through increased text and concept load, less reliance on visuals, longer sentences, and more literary language.

Level 4 builds reading stamina by providing more text per page, increased use of punctuation, greater variation in sentence patterns, and increasingly challenging vocabulary.

Level 5 encourages children to move from "learning to read" to "reading to learn" by providing even more text, varied writing styles, and less familiar topics.

Whichever book is right for your reader, Blastoff! Readers are the perfect books to build confidence and encourage a love of reading that will last a lifetime!

This edition first published in 2020 by Bellwether Media, Inc.

No part of this publication may be reproduced in whole or in part without written permission of the publisher. For information regarding permission, write to Bellwether Media, Inc., Attention: Permissions Department, 6012 Blue Circle Drive, Minnetonka, MN 55343.

Library of Congress Cataloging-in-Publication Data

Names: Shaffer, Lindsay, author.
Title: Clownfish / by Lindsay Shaffer.
Description: Minneapolis, MN : Bellwether Media, Inc., 2020. | Series: Animals of the coral reef | Includes bibliographical references and index. | Audience: Ages 5-8 (provided by Bellwether Media, Inc.) | Audience: Grades K-1 (provided by Bellwether Media, Inc.)
Identifiers: LCCN 2019033061 (print) | LCCN 2019033062 (ebook) | ISBN 9781618918130 (ebook) | ISBN 9781644871317 (library binding) | ISBN
Subjects: LCSH: Anemonefishes--Juvenile literature.
Classification: LCC QL638.P77 (ebook) | LCC QL638.P77 S53 2020 (print) | DDC 597/.72--dc23
LC record available at https://lccn.loc.gov/2019033061

Text copyright © 2020 by Bellwether Media, Inc. BLASTOFF! READERS and associated logos are trademarks and/or registered trademarks of Bellwether Media, Inc.

Editor: Betsy Rathburn   Designer: Laura Sowers

Printed in the United States of America, North Mankato, MN.

Table of Contents

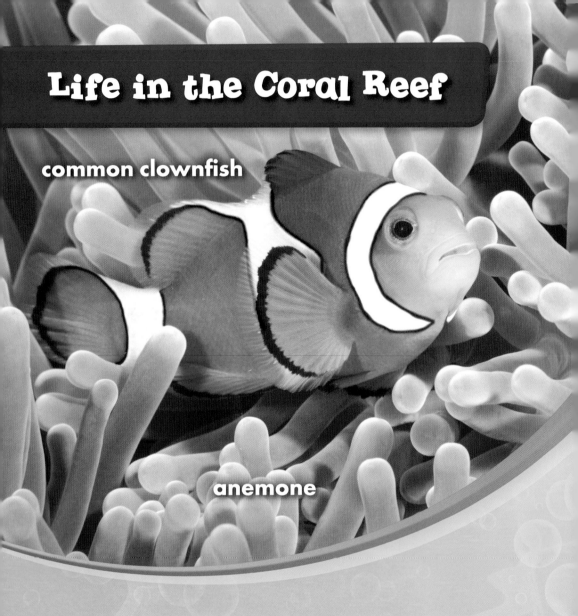

Life in the Coral Reef

common clownfish

anemone

Clownfish live in coral reefs of the Pacific and Indian Oceans.

The coral reef **biome** is full of **anemones**. Clownfish live inside them! They are often called anemonefish.

Common Clownfish Range

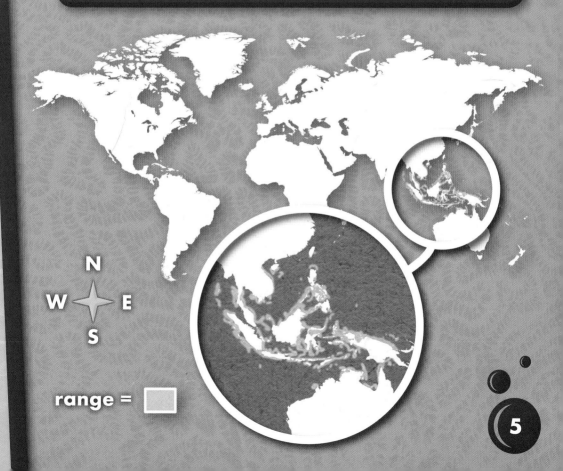

N
W E
S

range =

5

Anemones are **venomous**.
Stings from their **tentacles**
can kill most fish!

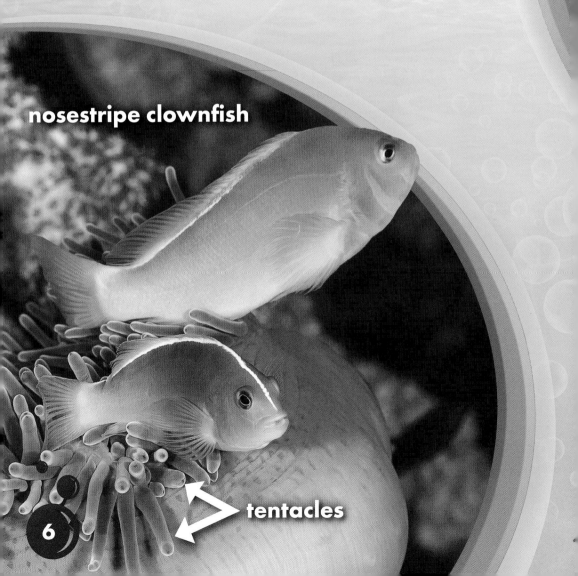

nosestripe clownfish

tentacles

But clownfish stay safe.
Mucus covers their skin.
It protects them from stings.

Coral reefs are full of **predators**. Clownfish must watch out for sharks and eels.

mucus on skin

round tail fin

Round tail fins help clownfish make sudden turns. This helps the fish escape!

Among the Tentacles

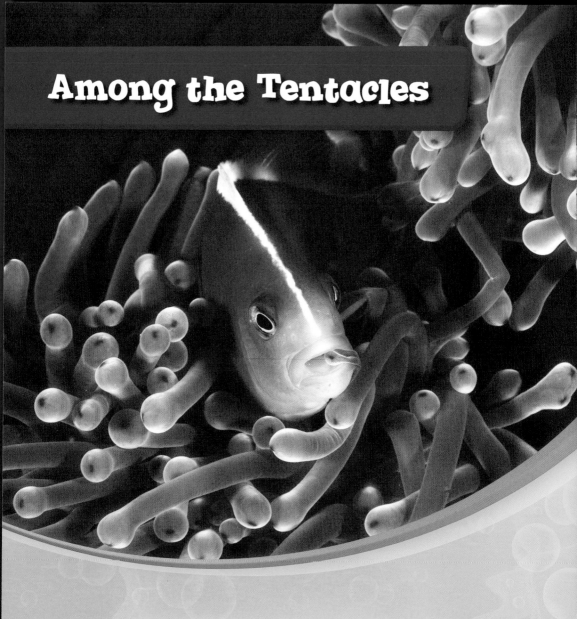

Anemones make homes
for clownfish. In return,
clownfish clean **parasites**
from anemone tentacles.

The fish also help
anemones grow.
Clownfish poop
acts as **fertilizer**!

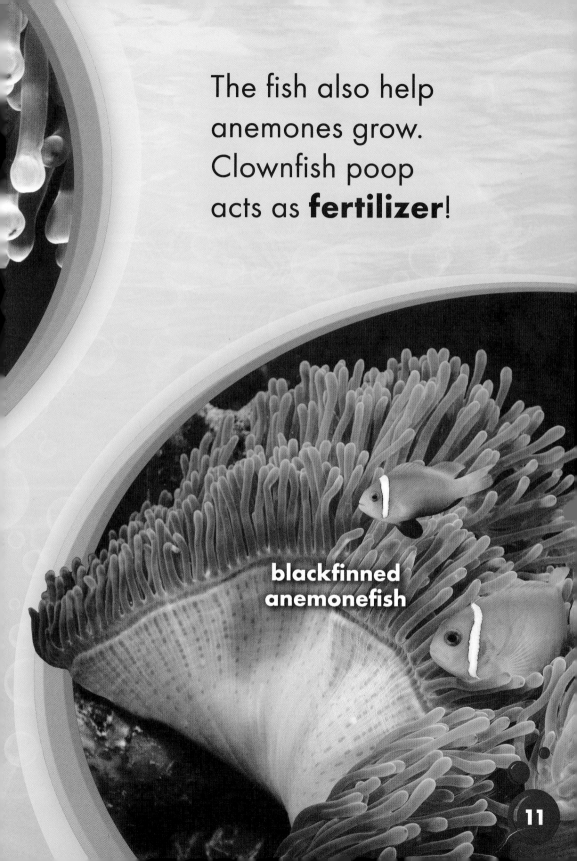

**blackfinned
anemonefish**

Some fish eat anemones.
Clownfish guard their
anemone homes.

They chase away fish
many times their own size!

Common Clownfish Stats

Least Concern	Near Threatened	Vulnerable	Endangered	Critically Endangered	Extinct in the Wild	Extinct

conservation status: least concern

life span: up to 10 years

Clownfish lay eggs to make babies. The eggs need a lot of care. Parents clean them.

saddleback clownfish

eggs

They wave their fins to move water around the eggs. This brings the eggs fresh **oxygen**!

Clownfish are **omnivores**. They eat plants and small **prey**.

They even eat parts of
the anemone they live in!

Clownfish **lure** other fish toward the anemone. Venomous tentacles sting the fish!

Clownfish Diet

algae

plankton

anemones

Clownfish eat the leftovers from the anemone's meal.

Coral reefs provide many different foods for clownfish.

These colorful fish
feel at home in the
coral reef biome!

Glossary

anemones—ocean animals with many long tentacles that sting their prey

biome—a large area with certain plants, animals, and weather

fertilizer—a material often made from animal poop that gives anemones nutrients

lure—to draw in

mucus—a clear liquid that covers the body of a clownfish

omnivores—animals that eat both plants and animals

oxygen—a gas that animals need to breathe

parasites—creatures that live on other living things and use them for food; parasites harm their hosts.

predators—animals that hunt other animals for food

prey—animals that are hunted by other animals for food

tentacles—long, bendable parts of an anemone

venomous—able to produce a poison called venom

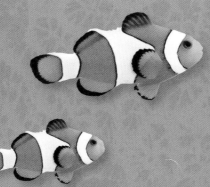

To Learn More

AT THE LIBRARY

Cunningham, Kevin. *Clownfish and Sea Anemones.* Ann Arbor, Mich.: Cherry Lake Publishing, 2017.

Laughlin, Kara L. *Clownfish.* Mankato, Minn.: Child's World, 2017.

Schuetz, Kari. *Clownfish and Sea Anemones.* Minneapolis, Minn.: Bellwether Media, 2019.

ON THE WEB

FACTSURFER

Factsurfer.com gives you a safe, fun way to find more information.

1. Go to www.factsurfer.com.

2. Enter "clownfish" into the search box and click 🔍.

3. Select your book cover to see a list of related web sites.

Index

The images in this book are reproduced through the courtesy of: Kletr, front cover (clownfish), p. 9; John_Walker, front cover (coral), pp. 2-3; cbpix, pp. 4-5, 17; Suwat Sirivutcharungchit, p. 6; fototrav, pp. 6-7; Krzysztof Bargiel, p. 8; Gaby Barathieu/ Getty Images, pp. 10-11; Richardom/ Alamy, p. 11; Jamesboy Nuchaikong, p. 12; Magnus Larsson, pp. 12-13; Michael Patrick O'Neill/ Alamy, p. 14; Jane Gould/ Alamy, pp. 14-15; National Geographic Image Collection/ Alamy, pp. 16-17; Jeff Rotman/ Alamy, pp. 18-19; Laura Dinraths, p. 19 (algae); Choksawatdikorn, p. 19 (plankton); John A. Anderson, p. 19 (anemones); Richard Whitcombe, pp. 20-21; Takashi Images, p. 21; Karel Kralovec, p. 22.